Dora's Box

Ann-Jeanette Campbell

∾

illustrated by Fabian Negrin

ALFRED A. KNOPF   NEW YORK

To Steve, who asked me to open Dora's box.
Requiescat in pace.—A.J.C.
To Ruy—F.N.

THIS IS A BORZOI BOOK PUBLISHED BY ALFRED A. KNOPF, INC.

Text copyright © 1998 by Ann-Jeanette Campbell
Illustrations copyright © 1998 by Fabian Negrin

http://www.randomhouse.com/

Library of Congress Cataloging-in-Publication Data
Campbell, Ann-Jeanette.
Dora's box / by Ann-Jeanette Campbell ; illustrated by Fabian Negrin.
p.   cm.
Summary: In order to protect her, Dora's parents put anything that might frighten or hurt her into a box and tell her never to open it, but when she eventually does, her life is enriched by what she finds.
ISBN 0-679-87642-1 (trade) — ISBN 0-679-97642-6 (lib. bdg.)
[1. Empathy—Fiction. 2. Emotions—Fiction. 3. Parent and child—Fiction.]
I. Negrin, Fabian, ill. II. Title.
PZ7.C15065Do   1998
[Fic]—dc21   97-6992

Printed in Singapore
10 9 8 7 6 5 4 3 2 1

First edition

One day, from the deepest, darkest, most frightening part of the forest, a man and a woman heard a painful cry. They ran toward the sound and found a dark and beautiful witch caught in a hunter's trap.

"If you release me," the witch cried, "I will grant you three wishes. But if you leave me, I will curse you with three oaths."

The man and the woman set her free. "We want to have a child," they said. That was their first wish. Their second wish was to protect their child from all that was evil or sad in the world. Their third wish was that their child would grow up to be loved by all.

"Those are very difficult wishes. I cannot make them come true all by myself, and they cannot come true all at the same time," said the witch. "This much I can do: I will give you a daughter and this box. This much you can do: Put in this box tokens of everything that is evil or sad in the world, and your daughter will never know them. If she opens the box, however, all your work will be undone.

"In the end, it is your daughter who must make your third wish come true. I will help her, but this much only *she* can do. You must be satisfied with this. Remember, you cannot have all three wishes at once."

The couple listened carefully to the witch's instructions, but in their excitement, they did not listen closely to her warnings.

Before long, their first wish came true. The man and the woman had a daughter. They named her Pandora, which means "all-giving," and called her Dora.

Soon after Dora was born, her mother took her out berry-picking. Insects buzzed in the air, and the thorny bushes scratched Dora's mother's arms, making her eyes fill with tears. She began to curse the berries and their thorns, but then remembered the box. She broke off a twig of the berry bush to put in the box, so Dora would never be scratched while picking berries.

One night, while Dora slept in her cradle, her father tended the fire. Not looking at what he was doing, he accidentally picked up a hot coal and burned his fingers. Just before he yelled out, he remembered the box. He carefully pulled the coal out of the fire and put it into the box, so Dora would never be burned by fire.

Every day and every night, Dora's mother and father gathered all the hurts, fears, angers, and frustrations they encountered and put them safely into Dora's box, so that she would never know them.

Dora grew up into a little girl who was always happy. She never got angry. She never pouted or was sad. She was never hurt by the sting of a bee, for her mother had put a bee's stinger in her box. She never felt afraid of a thunderstorm, because her father had gathered rain-soaked splinters from a tree struck by lightning and put them in the box.

But Dora never noticed how prettily a bee buzzed from flower to flower, and she never felt chills run down her spine when her father told ghost stories on stormy nights.

Dora liked the forest, especially the birds. But the birds thought there was something peculiar about the little girl who was never anything but happy. She didn't seem to be real flesh and blood. Only one bird, a dark and beautiful songbird, came to her window every morning to sing. Dora sang along with it, and, together, their voices could be heard through the forest.

One night, after Dora had gone to sleep, her mother and father heard a commotion. They ran outside and saw a red fox running away with something in its mouth. Startled, the fox dropped the tiny bundle. It was the songbird. The fox had killed it. Quickly, Dora's parents picked up the body of the bird, ran back inside, and put it in the box.

In the morning, when Dora woke up, she looked for the bird, but the sunlight in the forest caught her eye and she went out to play. She forgot all about her forest friend.

Soon after, a boy came to the house looking for his mother. They had been out walking, he said. He had run ahead and hidden behind a bush to surprise her. But she had not come. When he ran back to find her, she was gone. The little boy was frightened and lost, and he began to cry.

"Stop that," said Dora's mother, afraid that Dora might see. But the boy could not stop crying. "Give me your tears," she demanded, and she wiped them from the boy's cheeks with her thumbs. She sent him to play with Dora and quickly went to put his tears in Dora's box.

Dora and the boy played until suppertime. When the boy's mother still had not come by nightfall, Dora's mother put him to bed in Dora's room.

In the middle of the night, Dora woke up to a strange sound. She saw the boy sitting up in bed with his face hidden in his hands. He was making a terrible noise.

"What is the matter?" Dora asked.

"I am crying for my mother, but I do not have any tears, because your mother took them."

"I don't understand," said Dora, which was true. She did not know anything about crying or tears or missing mothers. "You have *my* mother. Isn't that good enough?" she asked.

"I want my own mother," said the boy, "and I want my tears back."

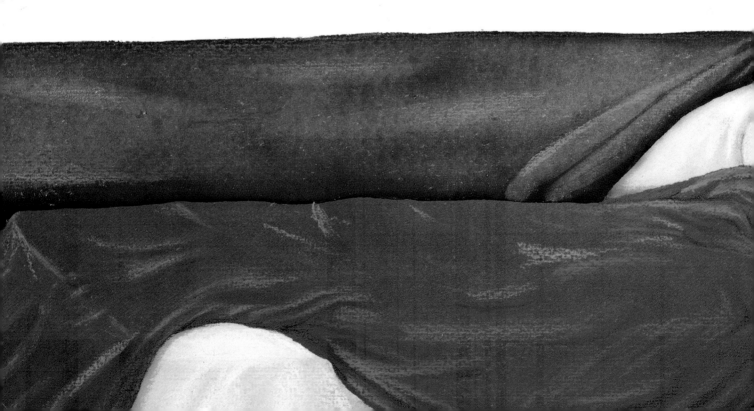

Dora wanted to make the boy stop crying, so she said that she would get his tears back for him, but he would have to show her where they were.

The moonlight shone through the living room windows. The boy pointed to a box on a high shelf. "That's where she put them," he said.

"But I am not allowed to touch that box," said Dora. "My mother and father have told me not to. They said that if I open it, I will wish I hadn't."

The boy put his hands to his face and began to cry again. Dora looked at him and then at the box. She would give the boy back his tears, she decided. She would open the box.

Dora pushed a chair over to the shelves. She could barely reach the box and had to stretch her fingers out to move it. But, finally, she held the box close to her. She put it on the floor near the fireplace and knelt in front of it.

Carefully, Dora lifted the lid with both hands. There, on top, were the boy's tears. Dora reached in and picked them up. As soon as she held them, she understood the boy's fear and sadness because he could not find his mother. After Dora gave the boy back his tears, he began to cry with them. She reached out to touch him, and, for the first time, she felt a little sad and frightened herself. When the boy's tears had dried up, she turned back to see what else was in the box.

Dora reached in again and again, and each time she picked something out of the box, she felt something she had never imagined before. She felt scratches from the berry bushes. She felt her fingers burn from the fire's hot coal. She felt the prick of a bee's sting and the fear of a thunderstorm. Everything came out of the box until there was just one thing left. Dora reached in and picked up the body of her little friend, the songbird.

Dora suddenly remembered how happy she had been every morning when she sang with her friend. For the first time, her own eyes filled with tears. They spilled out one after another and fell onto the little bird she held in her lap.

The moonlight was fading and the dawn's light beginning. Suddenly, the little body grew warm and began to breathe. Dora opened her hands and the bird flew to the window sill, where it opened its beak and trilled a morning song. Dora clapped her hands and sang back to her friend.

All the clapping and singing woke up Dora's parents, who rushed in to find Dora standing in the middle of the room, surrounded by everything they had carefully hidden in the box. The boy was gone, and in his place stood the dark and beautiful witch they had freed in the forest years before.

"All our work has been for nothing," Dora's parents cried. "What have you done? You have taken back our wish!"

"I fulfilled your wishes as I promised," said the witch. "I warned you when you made them that you could not have all three at once and that your daughter must make the third come true herself. Tonight, she has granted you your third wish. For, to be loved by all, she must have compassion, and to have compassion, she must know not only goodness and joy but also some of the evil and sadness in the world, as we all do."

From that day on, Dora grew up knowing
goodness and joy, and some evil and sadness,
and she was loved by all.